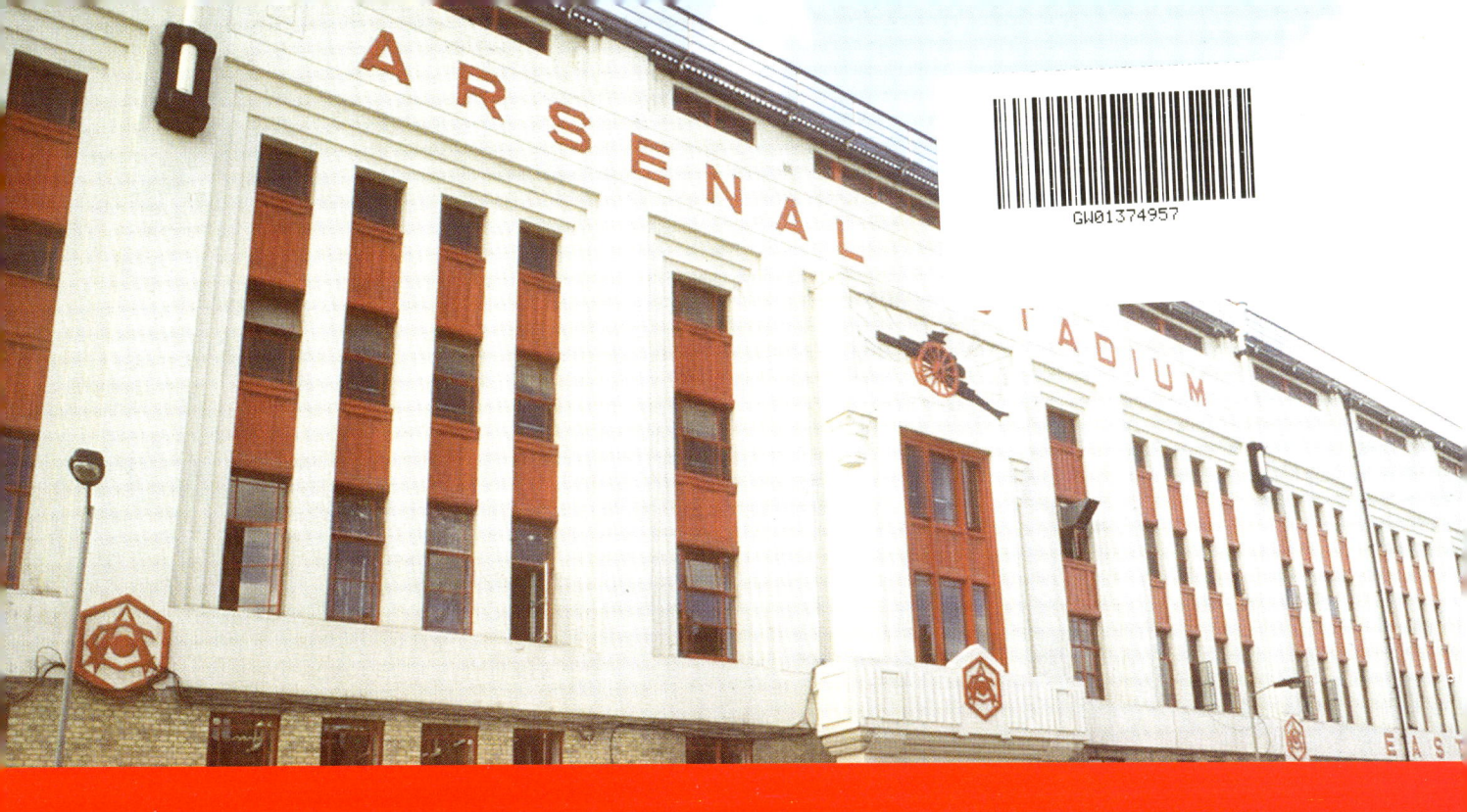

THE OFFICIAL
ARSENAL FC
English Book 1
Louis Fidge

Gunning for Goals

Education is essential to everyone and basic skills such as English and Maths are vitally important to every child's development.

Teaching core subjects through sport, I feel, is the best way. Encouraging youngsters to reach their goals in the classroom through Arsenal based activities is both a motivational and rewarding exercise.

That's why the Club already spearheads a number of successful education initiatives, including after school learning programmes at the Arsenal Study Support Centre and through the Arsenal 'Double Club'.

The inception of the Official Arsenal FC Workbook series further illustrates the Club's commitment to education. More importantly these books present an interesting and fun approach to learning at home.

I hope this book motivates you to accomplish your goals.

Arsène Wenger

Arsenal Study Support Centre
28 Carleton Road
London N7 0EQ
stevewilson@arsenalstudysupport.org
Telephone 020 7697 8467
Fax 020 7697 0873

Arsenal Double Club
Arsenal Stadium
London N5 1BU
bnicholas@arsenal.co.uk
Telephone 020 7704 4140
Fax 020 7704 4101

Kick-off

The Arsenal FC books are a fun way to learn and practise your English skills. Each book contains:
Theme visits to Arsenal FC, six Big Matches and a board game!

The 'theme' visits

Learn more about Arsenal FC and football.

Enjoy the fun activities (*answers on pages 30–31*).

The Big Matches

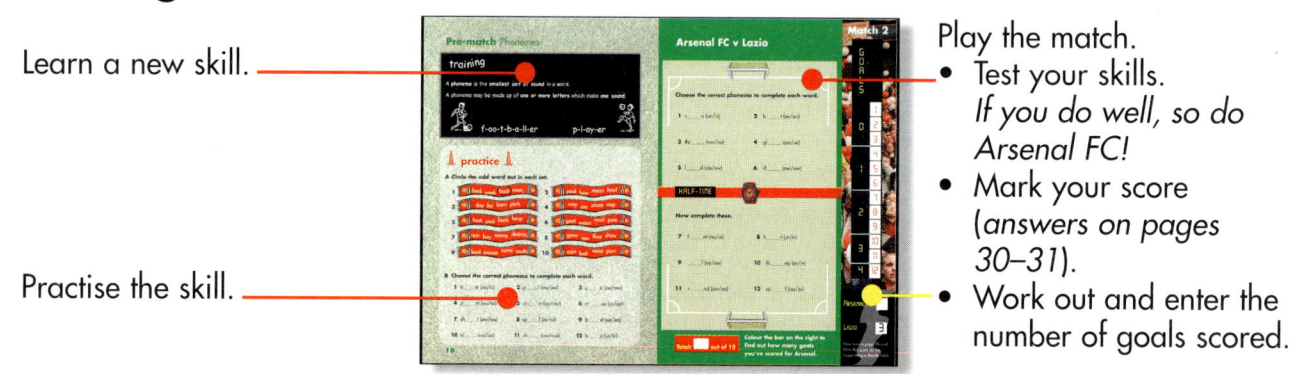

Learn a new skill.

Practise the skill.

Play the match.
- Test your skills. *If you do well, so do Arsenal FC!*
- Mark your score (*answers on pages 30–31*).
- Work out and enter the number of goals scored.

After the match:
Enter each result on page 28. Work out Arsenal FC's league position!

The board game

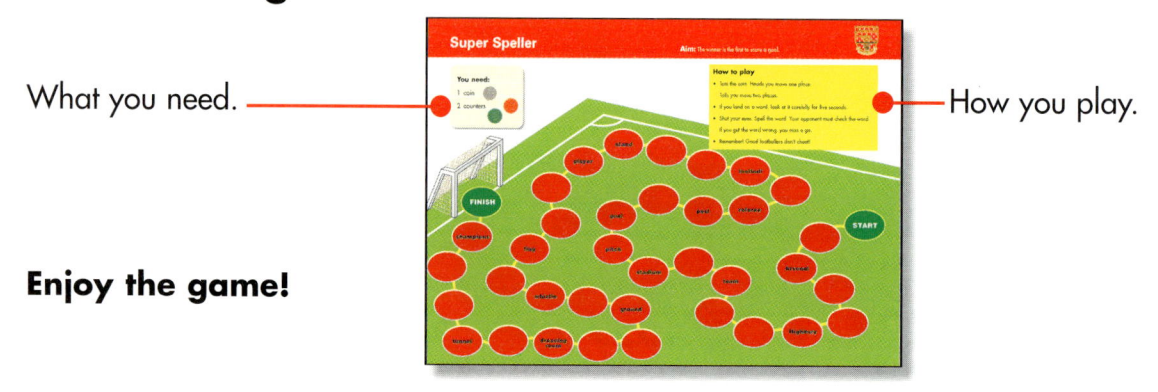

What you need.

How you play.

Enjoy the game!

Contents

	page		page
What's in a name?	4	**All in a day's work**	20
Match 1 Nouns	6	**Match 5** Singular and Plural	22
The Players	8	**The Museum**	24
Match 2 Phonemes	10	**Match 6** Silent Letters	26
The Strip	12	**Super-League Tables**	28
Match 3 Verbs	14	**Answers**	30
Super Speller	16	**Information**	32
Match 4 Prefixes	18		

What's in a name?

Arsenal have had several names since the team was started by workers at the Woolwich Arsenal Armament Factory in 1886. First they were called Dial Square (after one of the works premises), then Royal Arsenal. When they turned professional in 1891, they changed the name again to Woolwich Arsenal. They dropped the "Woolwich" soon after they moved to Highbury in 1913.

You will see the Arsenal name on many signs at Highbury.

3 How many words of four or more letters can you make from

Arsenal Football Club?

ARSENAL FOOTBALL CLUB
NOTICE BOARD

lean

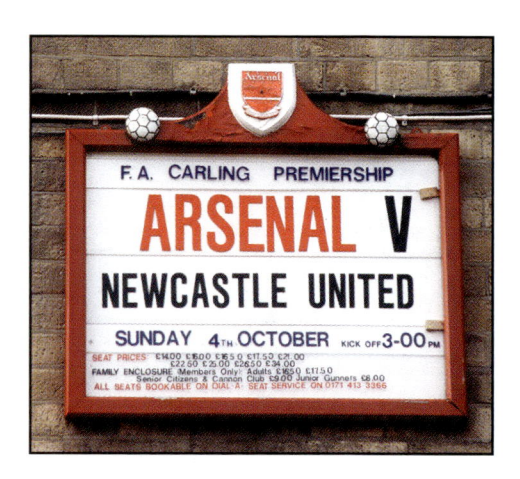

Finding hidden words.

1 How many words of two or more letters can you find hiding in **Dial Square**?

aid
_____
_____
_____
_____
_____
_____
_____

2 How many words of two or more letters can you find hiding in **Woolwich Arsenal**?

_____
_____
_____
_____
_____
_____
_____

An ACROSTIC is a word-puzzle where one word forms the initial letters of all the other words.

4 Finish the ACROSTIC on the scarf.

A
R gile
S ed-hot
E _____
N _____
A _____
L _____

F _____
C _____

5 Now make an ACROSTIC of your favourite player. Write the name on the scarf.

Pre-match Nouns

training

A **noun** is a **naming** word. It can be the name of a **person**, **place** or **thing**.

a supporter 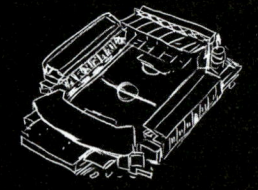   a stadium    a football

practice

A Match up each noun with its definition.

1	A FOOTBALLER	IS USED TO SEPARATE TWO PIECES OF LAND.
2	A PLUMBER	IS A PLACE WHERE BOOKS ARE KEPT.
3	A CLOWN	IS USED TO PUT LETTERS IN.
4	A FARM	PLAYS FOOTBALL.
5	A SHOP	IS USED TO DIG HOLES.
6	A LIBRARY	IS A PLACE WHERE CROPS CAN BE GROWN.
7	A FENCE	IS USED TO COOK FOOD IN.
8	A SPADE	MENDS BURST WATER PIPES.
9	AN ENVELOPE	IS A PLACE WHERE WE BUY THINGS.
10	A SAUCEPAN	MAKES US LAUGH.

B Circle the odd noun in each set.

1	horse	cow	bus	sheep
2	shoe	apple	orange	pear
3	onion	potato	carrot	guitar
4	chair	pen	table	bed
5	knife	fork	book	spoon
6	baker	farmer	lion	referee
7	ball	trumpet	piano	drums

Arsenal FC v Monaco

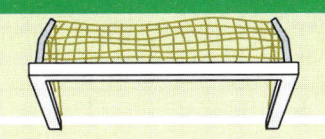

Match 1

Choose the correct noun to complete each sentence.

1. A _____ looks after the pitch. (steward/groundsman)
2. A _____ makes clothes. (tailor/grocer)
3. A _____ rides horses. (diver/jockey)
4. A _____ flies aeroplanes. (dentist/pilot)
5. You can get petrol from a _____ . (garage/church)
6. Aeroplanes fly from an _____ . (airport/abbey)

HALF-TIME

Now try these.

7. A horse lives in a _____ . (palace/stable)
8. You keep money in a _____ . (tree/bank)
9. We wash ourselves in a _____ . (bed/sink)
10. You watch football in a _____ . (stadium/cup)
11. Water is boiled in a _____ . (kettle/knife)
12. Clothes are kept in a _____ . (car/wardrobe)

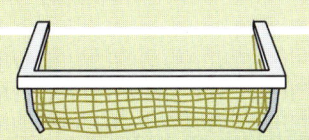

Total: ___ out of 12

Colour the bar on the right to find out how many goals you've scored for Arsenal.

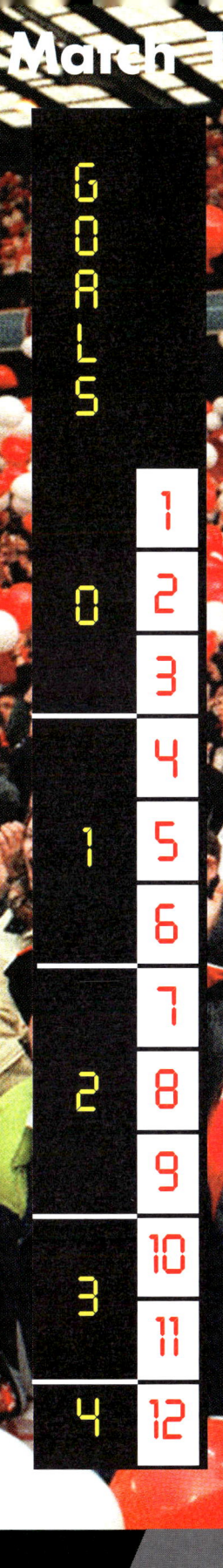

GOALS

Arsenal FC: 0
Monaco: 2

Now turn to page 28 and fill in the score on the Super-League Results Table.

The Players

Arsenal FC have some of the most famous players in the world. Thousands of people watch the team's matches and many will travel miles to see their favourite players in action.

Did you know ...?
The names of people are called *proper nouns*. They should always begin with a capital letter.

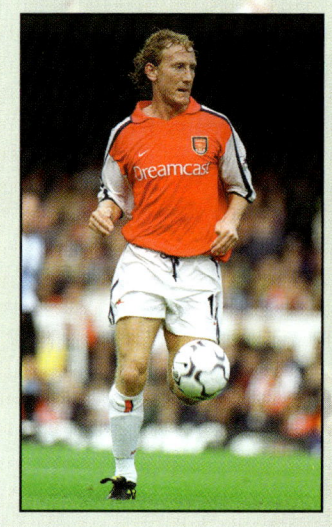

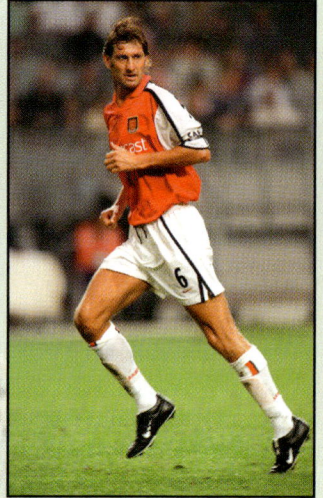

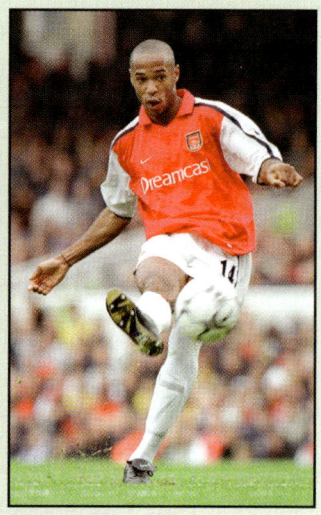

My Top Ten players.

3 Put the names of these players in alphabetical order.

1 Silvinho
2 Seaman
3 Adams
4 Kanu
5 Bergkamp
6 Vieira
7 Parlour
8 Henry
9 Dixon
10 Ljungberg

1 _____
2 _____
3 _____
4 _____
5 _____
6 _____
7 _____
8 _____
9 _____
10 _____

Using capital letters.

1 Write the names of the following players correctly:

   a fredrik ljungberg   b david seaman   c sylvain wiltord
   d kanu   e patrick vieira   f dennis bergkamp

   a _____   b _____   c _____
   d _____   e _____   f _____

2 Name the Arsenal players in the photos opposite.

   Write the name of each player correctly.   _____
                                                _____
                                                _____

4 Find the names of the ten players in this word-search football net.

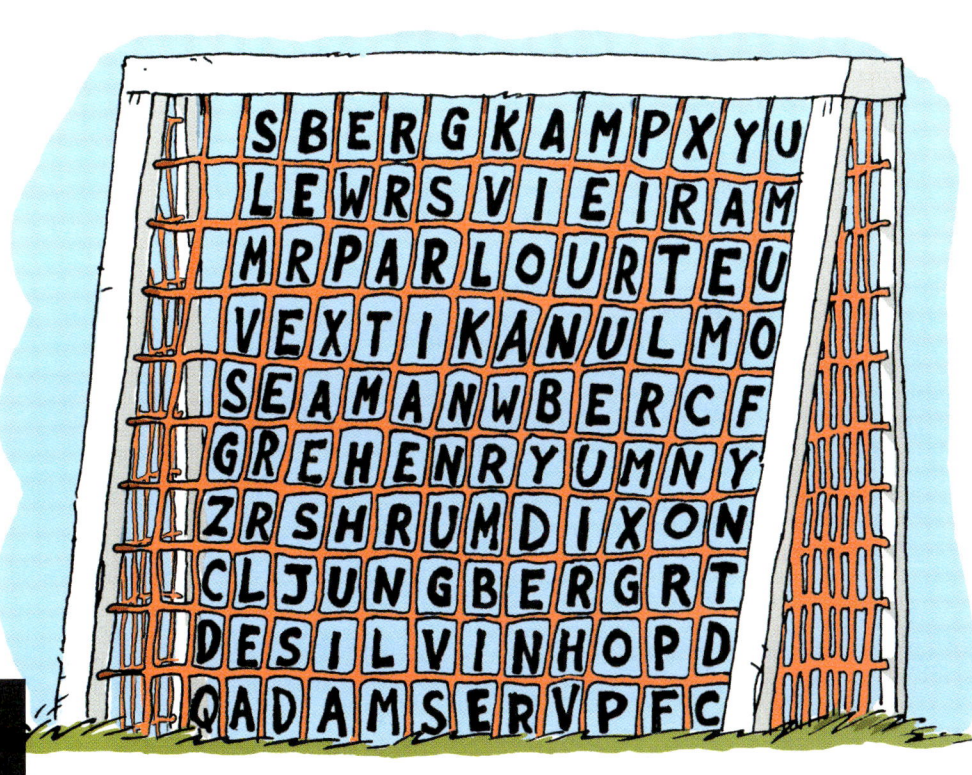

```
S B E R G K A M P X Y U
L E W R S V I E I R A M
M R P A R L O U R T E U
V E X T I K A N U L M O
S E A M A N W B E R C F
G R E H E N R Y U M N Y
Z R S H R U M D I X O N
C L J U N G B E R G R T
D E S I L V I N H O P D
Q A D A M S E R V P F C
```

EXTRA TIME

5 What is the name of Arsenal's number 10? _____

6 What is the name of Arsenal's manager? _____

9

Pre-match Phonemes

training

A **phoneme** is the **smallest unit of sound** in a word.

A phoneme may be made up of **one or more letters** which make **one sound**.

f-oo-t-b-a-ll-er   p-l-ay-er

practice

A Circle the odd word out in each set.

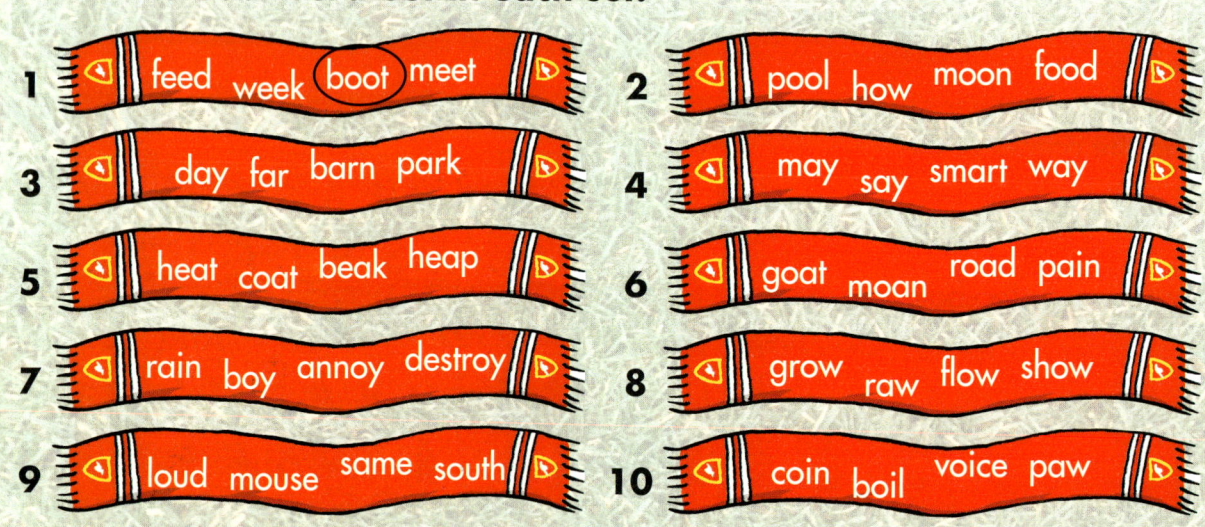

1. feed   week   (boot)   meet
2. pool   how   moon   food
3. day   far   barn   park
4. may   say   smart   way
5. heat   coat   beak   heap
6. goat   moan   road   pain
7. rain   boy   annoy   destroy
8. grow   raw   flow   show
9. loud   mouse   same   south
10. coin   boil   voice   paw

B Choose the correct phoneme to complete each word.

1. b____d (oo/ir)
2. p____l (oo/ow)
3. c____st (oa/ow)
4. p____nt (au/ai)
5. cr____n (ay/ow)
6. cr____on (ai/ay)
7. sh____t (ow/ou)
8. sp____l (oi/ai)
9. b____st (ee/ea)
10. bl____ (ue/oo)
11. sh____ (aw/ow)
12. b____n (ur/ir)

10

Arsenal FC v Lazio

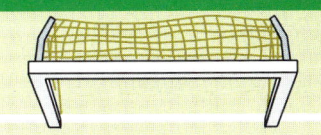

Match 2

Choose the correct phoneme to complete each word.

1. s____n (oo/ir)
2. h____t (ee/ea)
3. thr____ (ow/oo)
4. gl____ (oo/ue)
5. l____d (oa/ow)
6. cl____ (aw/ow)

HALF-TIME

Now complete these.

7. f____nt (au/ai)
8. h____t (ur/ir)
9. ____l (ay/ow)
10. th____sty (er/ir)
11. r____nd (ow/ou)
12. sp____l (oa/oi)

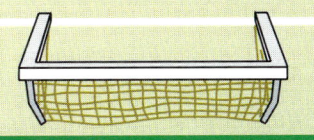

Total: ____ out of 12

Colour the bar on the right to find out how many goals you've scored for Arsenal.

GOALS

0
1
2
3
4

1
2
3
4
5
6
7
8
9
10
11
12

Arsenal FC ☐

Lazio 3

Now turn to page 28 and fill in the score on the Super-League Results Table.

The Strip

In the beginning, Arsenal had little money. Two players even asked Nottingham Forest to give them some of their shirts. This is why, back in 1886, their first strip was red. The white sleeves and collar were added in the 1930s.

1950

Some earlier Arsenal strips.

1 Here are some strips from the past. Match up the descriptions with the pictures of the old strips.

Here are the 2000–01 home, away and goalkeeper strips.

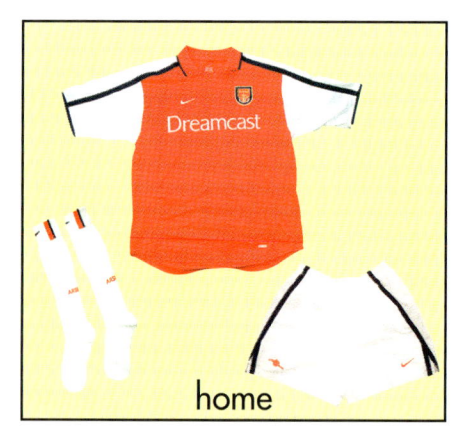

home

away

goalkeeper strip

2 Describe each strip in the chart.

	SHIRT	SHORTS	SOCKS
HOME			
AWAY			
KEEPER			

2	3	4
1971	1936	1970

a yellow shirt with white collar and white cuffs

b red shirt with white collar and white sleeves

c yellow shirt with blue trim on the neck and sleeves

d red shirt with a round white collar and white sleeves

3 Design your own Arsenal strip.

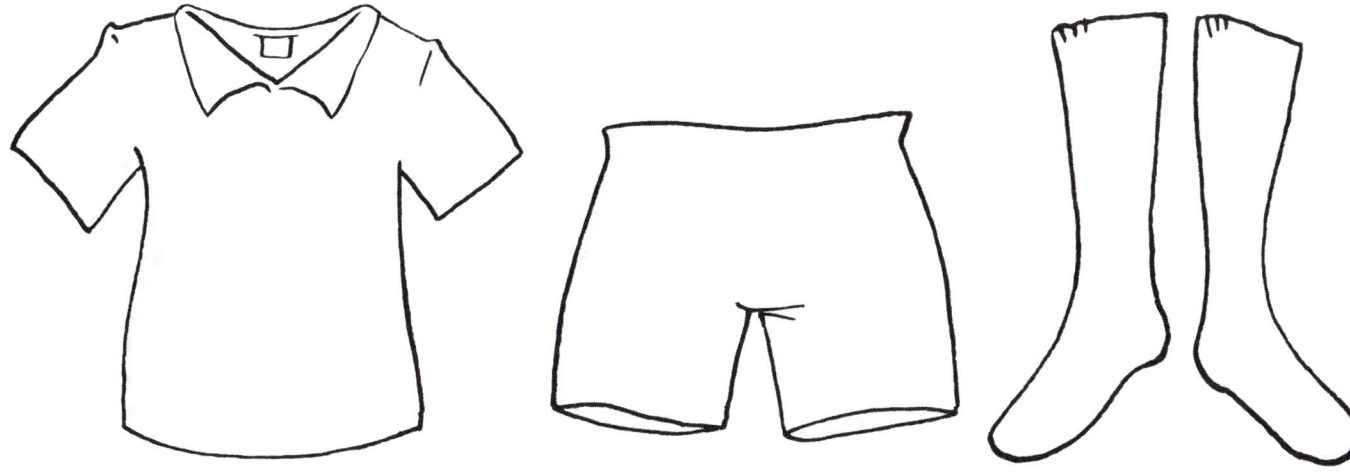

4 Write a description of your strip.

_____

_____

_____

13

Pre-match Verbs

training

A **verb** is an **action** word. It tells us what is **happening**.

The player **scored** a goal.

practice

Choose the correct verb to complete each of these sentences.

1 The winger _____ the ball.
2 The referee _____ the whistle.
3 The crowd _____ loudly.
4 The manager _____ the team.
5 My team _____ the Cup.
6 The captain _____ a throw-in.
7 The goalkeeper _____ the penalty.
8 The home team _____ Chelsea 1–0.
9 The defender _____ the centre-forward.
10 The team _____ in the Premier League.

ROARED
TOOK
PASSED
BEAT
PICKED
WON
TACKLED
SAVED
BLEW
PLAYED

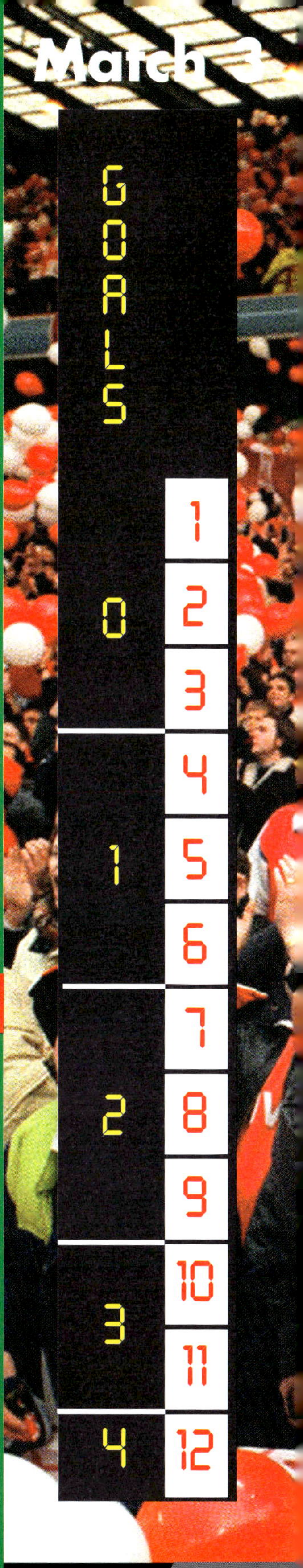

Arsenal FC v Valencia

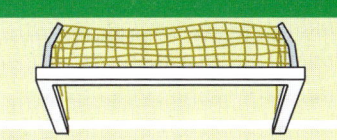

Match 3

Match up the pairs of verbs with similar meanings.

1	VANISH		SHOVE
2	PUSH		RACE
3	SPEAK		DISAPPEAR
4	RUN		SHUT
5	CLOSE		SWALLOW
6	DRINK		TALK

HALF-TIME

Now match these.

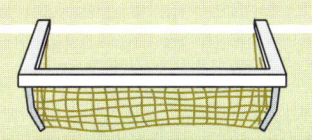

7	BRUSH		SKETCH
8	DRAW		BASH
9	MOAN		CONSUME
10	BANG		SWEEP
11	EAT		DOZE
12	SLEEP		GROAN

Total: ___ out of 12

Colour the bar on the right to find out how many goals you've scored for Arsenal.

GOALS

0	1
	2
	3
	4
1	5
	6
	7
2	8
	9
	10
3	11
4	12

ARSENAL FC ☐

VALENCIA 1

Now turn to page 28 and fill in the score on the Super-League Results Table.

Super Speller

You need:
- 1 coin
- 2 counters

FINISH

stand
player
goal
pitch
stadi[um]
ground
champions
flag
whistle
tunnel
dressing room

Aim: The winner is the first to score a goal.

How to play

- Toss the coin. Heads you move one place.

    Tails you move two places.

- If you land on a word, look at it carefully for five seconds.

- Shut your eyes. Spell the word. Your opponent must check the word.

    If you get the word wrong, you miss a go.

- Remember! Good footballers don't cheat!

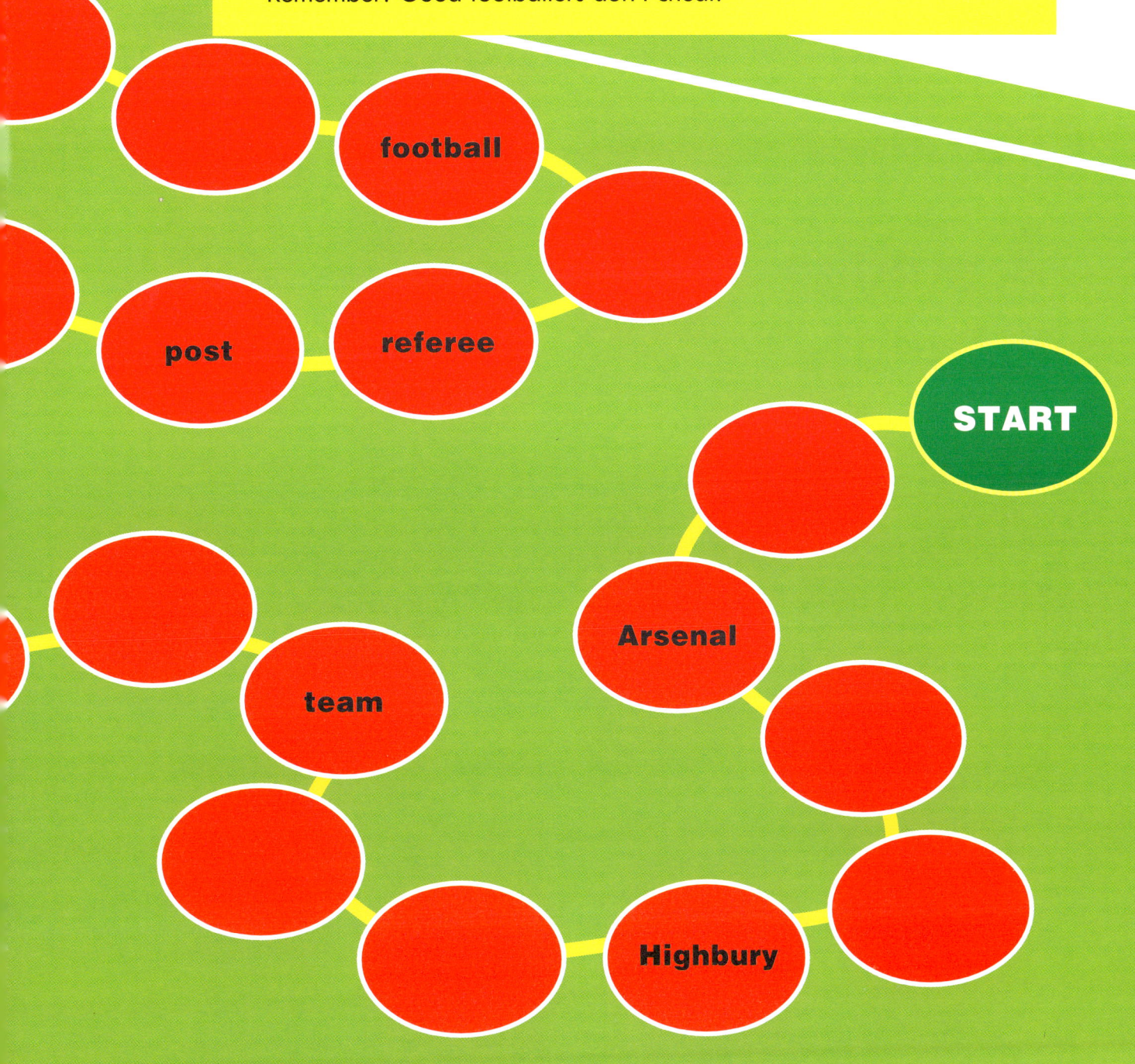

football

post

referee

START

Arsenal

team

Highbury

Pre-match Prefixes

training

A **prefix** is a group of letters we put **in front** of a word.

Prefixes **change the meaning** of a word.

happy   **un**happy

practice

Add the prefixes. Make some new words.

1 **un**   un___fair   ___well   ___pack

   unfair___   ___   ___

2 **dis**   ___agree   ___obey   ___honest

   ___   ___   ___

3 **re**   ___take   ___turn   ___place

   ___   ___   ___

4 **mis**   ___behave   ___judge   ___lead

   ___   ___   ___

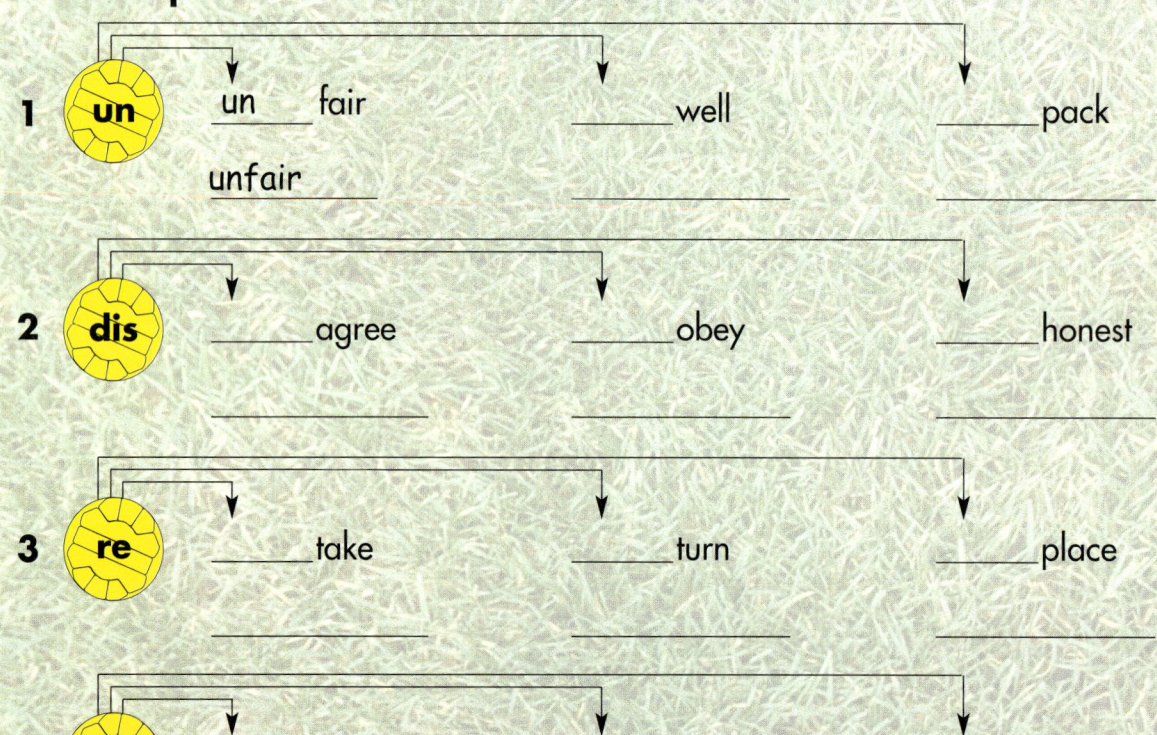

18

Arsenal FC v Bayern Munich

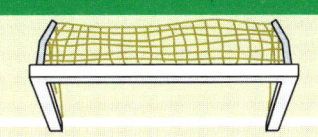

Match 4

Choose 'un' or 'dis' to complete each word.

1 _____ pack

2 _____ trust

3 _____ honest

4 _____ do

5 _____ happy

6 _____ allow

HALF-TIME

Choose 're' or 'mis' to complete each word.

7 _____ pay

8 _____ understand

9 _____ judge

10 _____ turn

11 _____ play

12 _____ behave

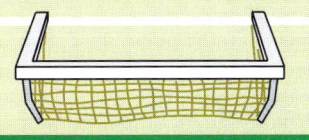

Total: ☐ **out of 12**

Colour the bar on the right to find out how many goals you've scored for Arsenal.

GOALS

Arsenal FC ☐

Bayern Munich 2

Now turn to page 28 and fill in the score on the Super-League Results Table.

All in a day's work

Here is a timetable of what happens on a typical day at Highbury.

match day timetable

7.00 am	The ground staff make sure the pitch is in tip-top condition.
10.00 am	The police and head stewards meet to plan their duties of ensuring crowd safety and making sure the fans behave well.
1.20 pm	The Arsenal players arrive.
1.30 pm	The away side arrives.
3.00 pm	Kick-off.
3.45 pm	Half time.
4.45 pm	The final whistle.
5.00 pm	The litter collectors clean up the ground and the surrounding streets.

The Arsenal players are famous for their football skills.

2 Write a short sentence under each picture to describe what each player is doing.

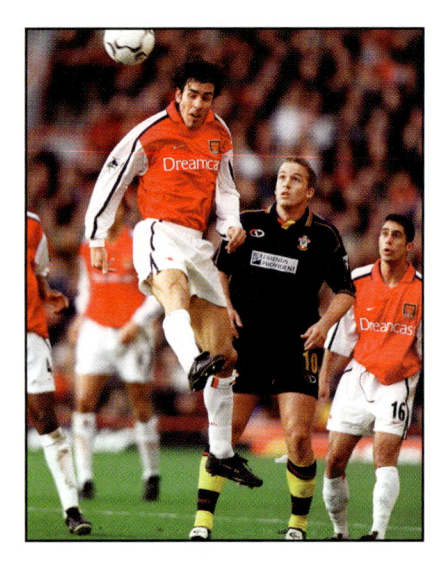

a _____

b _____

20

Are you as busy as the staff at Highbury on a Saturday?

1 Describe your normal Saturday.

7.00 am

10.00 am

12.00 pm

1.30 pm

3.00 pm

3.45 pm

4.45 pm

5.00 pm

c _____

d _____

21

Pre-match Singular and Plural

training

Nouns may be **singular** or **plural**.

Singular means **one**.   **Plural** means **more than one**.

one **fan**   lots of **fans**

practice

A Complete these charts.

	Singular	Plural
1	one ball	two _____
2	one goal	two _____
3	one bike	two _____
4	one brush	two _____

	Singular	Plural
5	one _____	two trees
6	one _____	two houses
7	one _____	two cars
8	one _____	two buses

B Now complete these charts. Take care with the spellings!

	Singular	Plural
1	one lady	two _____
2	one _____	two lorries
3	one thief	two _____
4	one _____	two loaves
5	one match	two _____

	Singular	Plural
6	one _____	two boxes
7	one potato	two _____
8	one _____	two tomatoes
9	one fox	two _____
10	one _____	two churches

Arsenal FC v Ajax

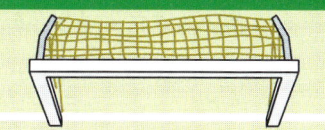

Match 5

GOALS

Arsenal: 0 / 1 / 2 / 3 / 4
Ajax: 1–12

Complete these plural nouns. Be careful with the spellings!

1. one chair, lots of _____
2. one box, lots of _____
3. one coach, lots of _____
4. one glass, lots of _____
5. one berry, lots of _____
6. one bush, lots of _____

HALF-TIME

Now complete these singular nouns.

7. one _____, lots of marbles
8. one _____, lots of dishes
9. one _____, lots of bunches
10. one _____, lots of copies
11. one _____, lots of volcanoes
12. one _____, lots of babies

Arsenal FC ☐
Ajax 1

Now turn to page 28 and fill in the score on the Super-League Results Table.

Total: ☐ out of 12

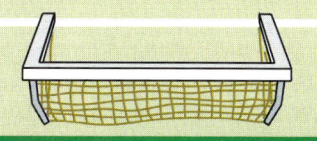

Colour the bar on the right to find out how many goals you've scored for Arsenal.

The Museum

When you go to Highbury you can visit the Arsenal Museum. The Museum is a celebration of the club's past, present and future. You can also have a tour of the dressing room and walk through the famous players' tunnel.

Now answer these questions about the Museum.

1 What memorabilia can be found in the Museum?

2 Explain what 'memorabilia' means. Use your dictionary to help you.

3 What is the Big Red Bus used for?

Here are a few treats to enjoy in the Museum.

ARSENAL

Big Red Bus
Displays Arsenal's trophies and parades around Islington.

Cinema
Up to 50 people can sit back and enjoy some of Arsenal's glory days.

Virtual Football
Try one of the Dreamcast machines that are in Highbury.

Quiz Station
You and your friends can see who has the most football knowledge.

Memorabilia
Shirts, boots, banners and pennants are all on display, including the shirts worn by Ian Wright, Dennis Bergkamp and Emmanuel Petit.

4 What does the quiz test you on?

5 What machines can you try out?

6 What can you see at the cinema?

25

Pre-match Silent Letters

training

Some words contain **silent letters**.

We cannot hear them when we say the words.

knot    thumb

practice

A Complete each of these words with 'b' or 'k'.

1 com____   2 thum____   3 ____nock
4 ____nee   5 ____now   6 clim____
7 crum____   8 ____not   9 ____night
10 ____nife   11 lam____   12 num____

B Complete each of these words with 'g', 'w' or 'l'.

1 ____rite   2 ____nome   3 ta____k
4 ____nash   5 ____reck   6 ____nat
7 ____rist   8 pa____m   9 cha____k
10 ca____f   11 ____naw   12 ca____m

26

Arsenal FC v Malmo

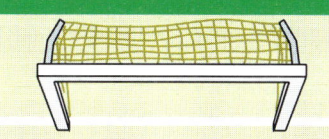

Match 6

Choose 'k' or 'w' to complete each word.

1. _____rite
2. _____nit
3. _____now
4. _____reck
5. _____rap
6. _____restle

HALF-TIME

Choose 'b' or 'g' to complete each word.

7. bom_____
8. lim_____
9. _____nome
10. _____nat
11. _____naw
12. clim_____

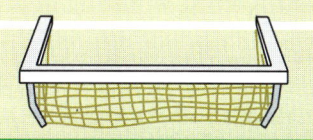

Total: _____ out of 12

Colour the bar on the right to find out how many goals you've scored for Arsenal.

GOALS
0
1
2
3
4

1
2
3
4
5
6
7
8
9
10
11
12

Arsenal FC ☐

Malmo 0

Now turn to page 28 and fill in the score on the Super-League Results Table.

Super-League Results

MATCH 1

Arsenal FC	☐	Monaco	2
Malmo	3	Valencia	2
Lazio	0	Ajax	2

MATCH 2

Arsenal FC	☐	Lazio	3
Valencia	2	Monaco	2
Malmo	2	B Munich	2

MATCH 3

Valencia	1	Arsenal FC	☐
Lazio	1	Monaco	0
Ajax	4	B Munich	3

MATCH 4

B Munich	2	Arsenal FC	☐
Valencia	1	Lazio	3
Malmo	0	Ajax	2

MATCH 5

Ajax	1	Arsenal FC	☐
B Munich	1	Lazio	1
Malmo	4	Monaco	0

MATCH 6

Arsenal FC	☐	Malmo	0
Monaco	0	Ajax	0
Valencia	0	B Munich	2

MATCH 7

B Munich	1	Monaco	3
Valencia	1	Ajax	1
Malmo	0	Lazio	1

28

Super-League Tables

Enter the score for each match.

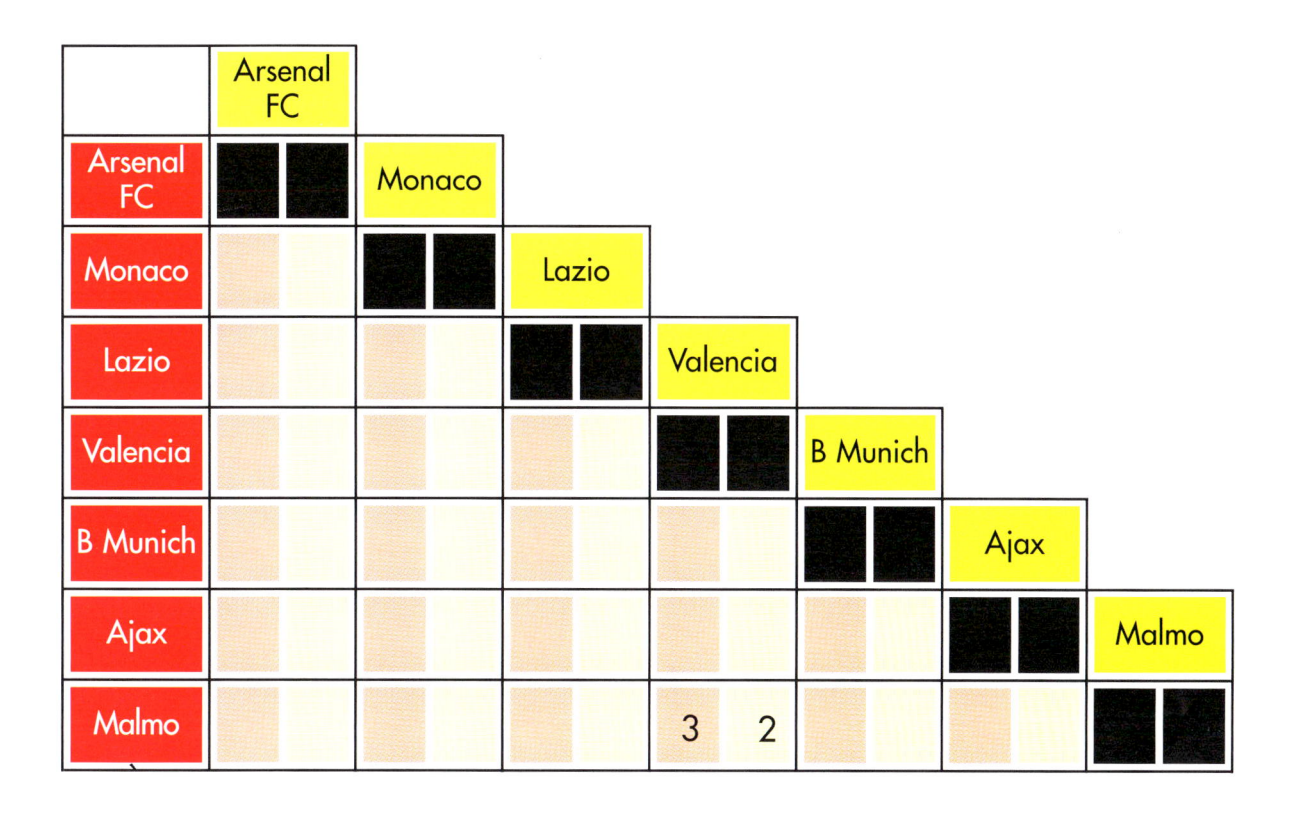

	Arsenal FC						
Arsenal FC	■ ■	Monaco					
Monaco		■ ■	Lazio				
Lazio			■ ■	Valencia			
Valencia				■ ■	B Munich		
B Munich					■ ■	Ajax	
Ajax						■ ■	Malmo
Malmo			3 2				■ ■

Complete the league table when all the matches are finished.

Win   3 pts   Draw   1 pt   Lose   0 pts

Team	Played	Won	Drew	Lost	For	Against	Goal diff	Points
Arsenal FC	6							
Monaco	6							
Lazio	6							
Valencia	6							
B Munich	6							
Ajax	6							
Malmo	6							

Champions ☐   Runners-up ☐

ANSWERS

What's in a name? 4–5
There may be other possible answers.
1 lad; red; squad; read; laid; sad; lid
2 wool; cool; whole; while; rain; lane; near; lean
3 leans; foot; near; ball; blot; bolt; tall; tool; lance; loot
4 (open)
5 (open)

Match 1 Nouns 6–7
Pre-match
A 1 A footballer plays football.
  2 A plumber mends burst water pipes.
  3 A clown makes us laugh.
  4 A farm is a place where crops can be grown.
  5 A shop is a place where we buy things.
  6 A library is a place where books are kept.
  7 A fence is used to separate two pieces of land.
  8 A spade is used to dig holes.
  9 An envelope is used to put letters in.
  10 A saucepan is used to cook food in.
B 1 bus 2 shoe 3 guitar 4 pen 5 book
  6 lion 7 ball

The Match
1 groundsman 2 tailor 3 jockey 4 pilot
5 garage 6 airport 7 stable 8 bank 9 sink
10 stadium 11 kettle 12 wardrobe

The Players 8–9
1 a Fredrik Ljungberg b David Seaman
  c Sylvain Wiltord d Kanu e Patrick Vieira
  f Dennis Bergkamp
2 Ray Parlour, Tony Adams, Thierry Henry
3 Adams, Bergkamp, Dixon, Henry, Kanu, Ljungberg, Parlour, Seaman, Silvinho, Vieira
4 Bergkamp, Vieira, Parlour, Kanu, Seaman, Henry, Dixon, Ljungberg, Silvinho, Adams
5 Dennis Bergkamp
6 Arsène Wenger

Match 2 Phonemes 10–11
Pre-match
A 1 boot 2 how 3 day 4 smart 5 coat
  6 pain 7 rain 8 raw 9 same 10 paw
B 1 bird 2 pool 3 coast 4 paint 5 crown
  6 crayon 7 shout 8 spoil 9 beast
  10 blue 11 show 12 burn

The Match
1 soon 2 heat 3 throw 4 glue 5 load
6 claw 7 faint 8 hurt 9 owl 10 thirsty
11 round 12 spoil

The Strip 12–13
1 a, c, b, d
2 (open)
3 (open)
4 (open)

Match 3 Verbs 14–15
Pre-match
1 passed 2 blew 3 roared 4 picked 5 won
6 took 7 saved 8 beat 9 tackled 10 played

The Match
1 vanish – disappear 2 push – shove
3 speak – talk 4 run – race 5 close – shut
6 drink – swallow 7 brush – sweep
8 draw – sketch 9 moan – groan
10 bang – bash 11 eat – consume
12 sleep – doze

Match 4 Prefixes 18–19
Pre-match
1 unfair unwell unpack
2 disagree disobey dishonest
3 retake return replace
4 misbehave misjudge mislead

The Match
1 unpack 2 distrust 3 dishonest 4 undo
5 unhappy 6 disallow 7 repay
8 misunderstand 9 misjudge 10 return
11 replay 12 misbehave

All in a day's work 20–21
1 (open)
2 (open)

30

Match 5 Singular and Plural 22-23

Pre-match
A **1** balls **2** goals **3** bikes **4** brushes **5** tree
   6 house **7** car **8** bus
B **1** ladies **2** lorry **3** thieves **4** loaf
   5 matches **6** box **7** potatoes **8** tomato
   9 foxes **10** church

The Match
1 chairs **2** boxes **3** coaches **4** glasses
5 berries **6** bushes **7** marble **8** dish
9 bunch **10** copy **11** volcano **12** baby

The Museum 24-25
1 Can find trophies, boots, shirts, banners, pennants.
2 It is memorable things. (Answers may vary)
3 It displays Arsenal's trophies and parades around Islington.
4 It tests your football knowledge.
5 You can try the Dreamcast virtual football.
6 You can see some of Arsenal's famous matches from the past.

Match 6 Silent Letters 26-27

Pre-match
A **1** comb **2** thumb **3** knock **4** knee **5** know
   6 climb **7** crumb **8** knot **9** knight
   10 knife **11** lamb **12** numb
B **1** write **2** gnome **3** talk **4** gnash **5** wreck
   6 gnat **7** wrist **8** palm **9** chalk **10** calf
   11 gnaw **12** calm

The Match
1 write **2** knit **3** know **4** wreck **5** wrap
6 wrestle **7** bomb **8** limb **9** gnome
10 gnat **11** gnaw **12** climb

Arsenal FC Double Club

The Double Club is an exciting new football and education venture developed by 'Arsenal in the Community'.

Inspired by Arsenal's Double 1998 League and Cup triumph, the Club involves 45 minutes of after school fun with literacy and numeracy study support and 45 minutes of football coaching.

Volunteers from local secondary schools help out with the Clubs.

Pupils complete a 24-week course to ensure that they receive the best tuition on and off the field.

If your primary, middle or secondary school is interested in receiving further information about the Double Club please contact Alan Sefton at: Arsenal Football Club
e-mail: bnicholas@arsenal.co.uk   Tel: 020 7704 4140   Fax: 020 7704 4001

Collect the set

Each book introduces new skills and harder challenges. Collect all 8 and be an English and Maths champion.

Arsenal FC English Books 1-4

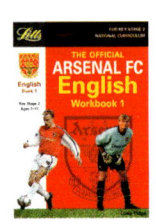

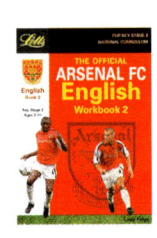

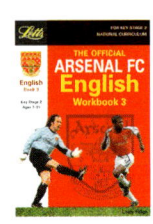

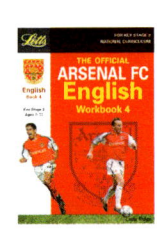

Arsenal FC Maths Books 1-4

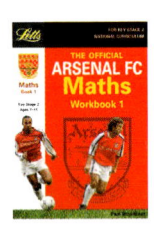

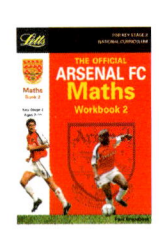

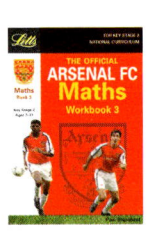

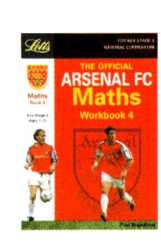

For all the latest news, views and information on

Arsenal FC

visit the official Arsenal website:

www.arsenal.com

Arsenal Football Club PLC
Arsenal Stadium, Highbury, London N5 1BU

Letts Educational, Aldine House, Aldine Place, London W12 8AW
Tel: 020 8740 2266 Fax: 020 8743 8451 E-mail: mail@lettsed.co.uk
Website: www.letts-education.com

Every effort has been made to trace copyright holders and obtain their permission for the use of copyright material. The authors and publishers will gladly receive information enabling them to rectify any error or omission in subsequent editions.

All facts are correct at time of going to press.

Published 2001
© Letts Educational Ltd
Author: Louis Fidge
Editorial and Design: Moondisks Ltd, Cambridge
Illustrations: Joel Morris
Colour Reprographics: PDQ Digital Media Solutions Ltd, Bungay

Our thanks to the players and staff at Arsenal Football Club.
Photographs copyright Arsenal Football Club and Colorsport.

All rights reserved. No part of this publication may be reproduced, stored in a retrieval system, or transmitted, in any form or by any means, electronic, mechanical, photocopying, recording or otherwise, without the prior permission of Letts Educational.

British Library Cataloguing in Publication Data
A CIP record for this book is available from the British Library.
ISBN 1-85805-883-X

Printed in the UK.

Letts Educational Limited is a member of Granada Learning Limited, part of the Granada Media Group.